A Patient Desire

NEW POEMS

Praise for *A Patient Desire*

"This first gathering of lyrical works from poet Tim Nonn's journey into his oncoming blindness is sometimes beautiful, other times astonishingly wise. When he says 'going blind/is another way/of seeing/the heart clearly,' he accepts the dare of kinship with Rumi and Basho, Roethke and Bly, a lineage of mystics and, perhaps ironically, seers. His unrhymed quatrains, deceptively simple, are fully armed with axioms: 'knowing is impossible/you must feel your way/into your heart/and get lost.' And his mastery of simple means as an approach to the ineffable is always in effect, as when 'in the presence/of a tree/stillness/is a conversation' or 'an evening song/of a bird facing darkness/had the lonely clarity/of one in love with light.' One in love with the light indeed. Here Tim Nonn welcomes you and it is likely you will find yourself happily entranced."

—William Pitt Root, author of *Strange Angels, Striking the Dark Air for Music*, etc.

"What is it to truly see? Timothy Nonn answers this philosophical question in *A Patient Desire*, his collection of haiku-like poems. Ironically, Nonn has learned what it is to truly see as a result of his own loss of sight. The five segments of the book—*Opening, Creekwalking, A Conspiracy of Trees, Breath and Tea*, and *Becoming Love*—take us on a poignant yet zen-like walk through life with courage and grace: 'going blind /is another way/of seeing/the heart clearly' and 'in winter trees/let go of their leaves/trusting the sanctuary/of darkness.' Trust in Nonn's leadership and learn to see, and become love."

—Armando García-Dávila, 2002 Healdsburg Literary Laureate, and author of *Profile: Poems & Stories*, and the novel *The Trip*.

A Patient Desire

NEW POEMS

TIMOTHY NONN

MCCAA BOOKS • SANTA ROSA

McCaa Books
1604 Deer Run
Santa Rosa, CA 95405-7535

Copyright © 2017 by Timothy Nonn
All Rights Reserved

Without limiting the rights under copyright reserved above, no part of this publication may be reproduced, distributed, or transmitted in any form or by any means, or stored in a database or retrieval system, without the prior written permission of both the copyright owner and the publisher of this book except in the case of brief quotations embodied in critical articles or reviews.

ISBN 978-0-692-84272-0

First published in 2017 by McCaa Books,
an imprint of McCaa Publications.

Printed in the United States of America
Set in Minion Pro

Cover photo by Daphne Shapiro
Cover and book layout by Waights Taylor Jr.

www.mccaabooks.com

Dedication

To my son, Jonathan.

CONTENTS

Preface   11

A Patient Desire 15

Poems Set to a Theme
Opening 17
Creekwalking 45
A Conspiracy of Trees 79
Breath and Tea 119
Becoming Love 139

Acknowledgments 173
About the Poet 175

PREFACE

Going blind led me back into poetry in a completely new way. I started to pay attention to little things each day, in part, just so I wouldn't fall over on my face. But as I paid attention to ordinary things, I started to discover beauty in unexpected places: an old teapot, a breath, even darkness. Here is a little meditation I wrote on the rain.

Tonight, the rain is coming down hard. While listening to it, I realized my partial blindness wasn't an obstacle to listening to rain. I probably couldn't see the raindrops even if I had 20/20 vision. So I closed my eyes and practiced being completely blind while listening.

The sound of rain immediately became richer and more complex as I listened in darkness. It had a beautiful and immense diversity of voices. And though I couldn't hear every note of every raindrop, I heard many of them. The ones falling on leaves and bushes, on roofs and concrete patios, and on grass and puddles.

Opening my eyes, I knew I would carry this intimate encounter with rain into my complete blindness. It felt like a path leading from one place to another. It was less frightening, even comforting, to know that in darkness from time to time the rain will sing and I will listen.

I began writing four-line poems without punctuation when it became impossible for me to see the punctuation marks on the keyboard. Four-line poems are very easy for me to memorize too. Sometimes I will spend hours on a four-line poem with seven or nine words.

For many people, this would seem like a terrible waste of time. But my poems are the way I meditate. Meditation can occur by sitting quietly, walking or lying down. Focusing on one poem for a long period of time enables me to feel connected to the beauty and love within and around us. Each word becomes critically important.

This method has taught me a deep love of words. To see them as living. When I get a poem right, I can feel it in my whole body. It's an ecstatic experience. So it's no coincidence that many of my poems come out of dance, which I do for several hours every night.

I invite you to spend some time with the poems you connect with. Use them to connect with the deepest parts of your own experience. Hopefully, they will come alive and you will come alive in unexpected ways.

Timothy Nonn
March 2017

A Patient Desire

when the branches
of a tree
reach into emptiness
and touch light

when the roots
of a tree
reach into darkness
and taste water

when the leaves
of a tree
feel the wind
and together sing

when the bark
of a tree
swells with rain
and turns fragrant

when the trunk
of a tree
draws you closer
into its stillness

there I am
always with you
here between us
a patient desire

Opening

Opening

even a tiny window
opens to the vast sky
and my heart
to the infinitude of love

Opening

what a world
growing beauty
everywhere
for any excuse

Opening

open a window
there is a bird outside
waiting to sing
for you

Opening

in the silence
between the singing
of a mourning dove
my heart awakened

Opening

my heart is a wilderness
where I roam free
everywhere I look
your presence nourishes me

Opening

how you see
with an open
or closed heart
creates the world

Opening

finding
the rhythm of love
within yourself
is to find it everywhere

Opening

two choices
love or fear
we grow
what we plant

Opening

darkness comes slowly
giving dusk a chance
to play with the light
one last time

Opening

going blind
is another way
of seeing
the heart clearly

Opening

an evening song
of a bird facing darkness
had the lonely clarity
of one in love with light

Opening

listen
the rain is singing
like the rustling skirt
of a dancing goddess

Opening

I wring meaning
from small things
my universe box
is open

Creekwalking

Creekwalking

creekwalking
is the practice
of wandering
aimlessly through stillness

Creekwalking

walking by the creek
I placed my hand
on a tree trunk
and felt the heart of stillness

Creekwalking

following the creek
without a destination
is the only way
to find where you are going

Creekwalking

croaking frogs
hiding in grass
along the creek
greet the evening

Creekwalking

on a walk
by the creek
the dog leapt with joy
for no apparent reason

Creekwalking

let love lead you
wherever it wants
to walk with you
even along a dry creek

Creekwalking

night winds
brought rain
soft scented arms
held me

Creekwalking

golden leaves
fell beautifully
drifting away
along the creek

Creekwalking

children shout
in the rain
frogs croak
in new mud

Creekwalking

catching the scent
of dogs
a squirrel leapt
to a higher branch

Creekwalking

here we walk
embraced by earth
breathing skies
listening to geese

Creekwalking

short rain
lone frog
croaking
under a redwood

Creekwalking

find a bird
who will sing to you
and listen
with the heart of the universe

Creekwalking

along the dry creek
a scent of eucalyptus
rose like prayers for rain
as wildfires burned

Creekwalking

on the path
along the creek
a bird sang
a new song

Creekwalking

it comes at the perfect time
but it was always there
waiting for you to see
wildflowers at your feet

A Conspiracy of Trees

A Conspiracy of Trees

in the presence
of a tree
stillness
is a conversation

A Conspiracy of Trees

you have to be quiet
to listen to trees
experience their joy
leaf by leaf

A Conspiracy of Trees

branches reach into sky
roots reach into earth
trees know
where love grows

A Conspiracy of Trees

a tree holds
the earth and sky
with the stillness of hearts
opening together

A Conspiracy of Trees

I work at perfecting
my relationship
with trees
silently

A Conspiracy of Trees

each tree
holds a space
of earth and sky
a sanctuary with roots

A Conspiracy of Trees

winter is letting go
of dry leaves
a time to trust
in the nakedness of limbs

A Conspiracy of Trees

escaping fog
the moon
perched precariously
on a hemlock branch

A Conspiracy of Trees

a tree thinks
with its leaves
telling stories
to the wind

A Conspiracy of Trees

how long does it take
to fall in love with a tree
to feel the intimacy of stillness
joining our hearts as one

A Conspiracy of Trees

I pray with my heart
pressed against a tree
not asking for anything
only the scent of bark

A Conspiracy of Trees

in winter trees
let go of their leaves
trusting the sanctuary
of darkness

A Conspiracy of Trees

approaching the stillness
of a redwood tree
it draws me closer
whispering secrets

A Conspiracy of Trees

leaning tree
perfectly imperfect
leaping toward
a thousand suns

A Conspiracy of Trees

stillness rises
from the earth
through branches
radiant with moonlight

A Conspiracy of Trees

why do you ask me
to live in fear
when all the leaves
are changing color

A Conspiracy of Trees

wind practices
touching leaves
turning caresses
into song

A Conspiracy of Trees

seven trunks growing from one
glistened in the cold winter rain
shining with infinite stars
in the deepening darkness

A Conspiracy of Trees

Thou light
 each leaf whispers
Thou wind
 in a chorus of colors

Breath and Tea

Breath and Tea

find the ocean
in a single raindrop
and your life
in a single breath

Breath and Tea

slow down
to the pace
of compassion
when hearts see together

Breath and Tea

some days a time comes
when a space opens up
out of nowhere
and just breathing is bliss

Breath and Tea

solitude is a practice
take a breath
of life
and another

Breath and Tea

listen to the earth
breathe her beauty
until your heart
flowers

Breath and Tea

in the space
where things fall apart
making tea
is ending and beginning

Breath and Tea

a pot of tea
offered its fragrance
for a moment
the world smelled sweet

Breath and Tea

beauty is a physical act
turning breath to song
touch to love
our bodies create us

Breath and Tea

every step we take
is a memory of earth
from our touch
sighs of roses

Becoming Love

Becoming Love

becoming love
is a dance
our bodies
teach us

Becoming Love

knowing is impossible
you must feel your way
into your heart
and get lost

Becoming Love

in the wilderness
of love
nothing is familiar
paths grow like grass

Becoming Love

our power
to love
turns us
inside out

Becoming Love

we hold the pain
of the earth
knowing
its love holds us

Becoming Love

winter empties
our hearts
in the darkness
we become light

Becoming Love

I tried to hide
deep inside
but you found me
with one look

Becoming Love

our lips touched
and I tasted
a thousand rivers
in your heart

Becoming Love

you let me
sit by you
we spoke and
silence healed us

Becoming Love

the hard part
of letting go
is learning
to embrace

Becoming Love

you will never know
if your heart
is a door to the universe
until you open it

Becoming Love

in the middle of talking
you sang a sentence
it was startling
to see you so beautiful

Becoming Love

when you hold me
in your stillness
we become
wilderness

Becoming Love

for so long
it was out there
now it is in here
abundantly

Becoming Love

just because
I have this heart
opening in broad daylight
does not mean you see me

Breath and Tea

all the love
that ever was
is here now
in our hearts

Acknowledgments

This book would not have come to pass had it not been for Waights Taylor Jr. His encouragement and patience were invaluable.

I am indebted to the fine writers whose work I admire for taking the time to review and comment on my work.

William Pitt Root is an internationally acclaimed poet and editor. A list of his many books of poetry and awards would overflow this page. He received fellowships from the Rockefeller Foundation, the Guggenheim Foundation, the National Endowment for the Arts, and a Stegner Fellowship at Stanford University.

Armando García-Dávila is a poet and author. His poems have been widely published and also found their way into union newsletters and Sunday pulpits. He has read his poetry to immigrant laborers in the vineyards and prisoners in San Quentin. In 2002, he was chosen as the Healdsburg Literary Laureate. His first novel, *The Trip*, is scheduled for publication in early 2017.

About the Poet

Tim Nonn is single father living in Rohnert Park, California. He has a Masters of Divinity from San Francisco Theological Seminary and a doctorate in ethics from the Graduate Theological Union. He worked as an organizer for several decades in global human rights movements.

In the 1980s, he was a founder of the Sanctuary movement, which provided safe haven for hundreds of high risk refugees fleeing civil wars and persecution in Central America and led to the creation of dozens of sanctuary cities throughout the United States.

From 2004 to 2008, he was a national organizer for a movement to end the genocide in Darfur, Sudan.

Currently, he is a school board member of the Cotati-Rohnert Park Unified School District. He retired in 2012 to devote himself to writing. He finished his first novel, *The Black Prison*, last year. His favorite pastimes are walking along the creeks in his hometown and dancing.

www.ingramcontent.com/pod-product-compliance
Lightning Source LLC
Chambersburg PA
CBHW051833090426
42736CB00011B/1787